P9-DTL-500

ANCIENT GHANA

THE KINGDOMS OF AFRICA

ANCIENT GHANA

THE LAND OF GOLD

PHILIP KOSLOW

CHELSEA HOUSE PUBLISHERS • New York • Philadelphia

Frontispiece: An engraving from Mungo Park's *Travels in the Interior Districts of Africa* (1799).

On the Cover: An artist's rendering of a terra-cotta head from Nok in Central Nigeria; in the background, the artist's interpretation of a landscape in the territory of ancient Ghana.

CHELSEA HOUSE PUBLISHERS

Editorial Director Richard Rennert
Executive Managing Editor Karyn Gullen Browne
Copy Chief Robin James
Picture Editor Adrian G. Allen
Art Director Robert Mitchell
Manufacturing Director Gerald Levine
Assistant Art Director Joan Ferrigno

THE KINGDOMS OF AFRICA
Senior Editor Martin Schwabacher

Staff for ANCIENT GHANA
Assistant Editor Catherine Iannone
Editorial Assistant Sydra Mallery
Designer Cambraia Magalhães
Picture Researcher Sandy Jones
Cover Illustrator Bradford Brown

First Printing
1 3 5 7 9 8 6 4 2

Library of Congress Cataloging-in-Publication Data

Koslow, Philip.
  Ancient Ghana: the land of gold/Philip Koslow
    p. cm.—(The Kingdoms of Africa)
Includes bibliographical references and index.
  ISBN   0-7910-3126-8.
          0-7910-2941-7 (pbk.)

  1. Ghana—History—To 1957—Juvenile literature. [1. Ghana—History.]
I. Title. II. Series.
DT511.K68 1995
966.7—dc20

94-26192
CIP
AC

CONTENTS

Titles In
THE KINGDOMS OF AFRICA

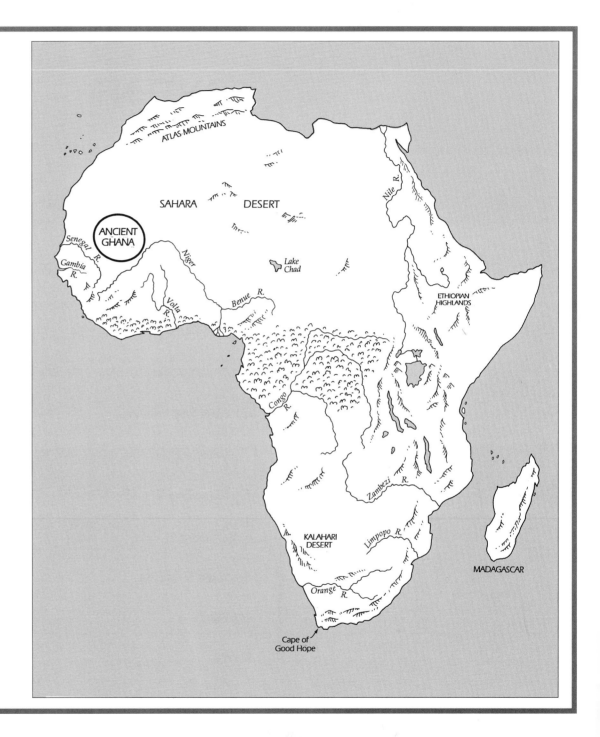

"CIVILIZATION AND MAGNIFICENCE"

On a sunny morning in July 1796, Mungo Park, a Scottish doctor turned explorer, achieved a major goal of his long and difficult trek through West Africa when he reached the banks of the mighty Niger River. Along the river was a cluster of four large towns, which together made up the city of Segu. The sight of these settlements dazzled Park as much as the spectacle of the broad, shining waterway. "The view of this extensive city," he wrote, "the numerous canoes upon the river; the crowded population; and the cultivated state of the surrounding country, formed altogether a prospect of civilization and magnificence, which I little expected to find in the bosom of Africa."

Park's account of his journey, *Travels in the Interior Districts of Africa*, became a best-seller in England. But his respectful assessment of the citizens of Africa was soon brushed aside by the English and other Europeans, who were engaged in a profitable trade in slaves along the West African coast and would eventually carve the entire continent into colonies. After Park drowned during a second expedition to Africa in 1806, later explorers such as Richard Burton achieved great fame by writing of the "childishness" and "backwardness" of Africans. Their views became the accepted wisdom in Europe, even among academics.

One hundred years after Park's arrival at Segu, a professor at Oxford University in England wrote with bland self-assurance that African history before the arrival of Europeans had been nothing more than "blank, uninteresting, brutal barbarism."

A relief map of the continent of Africa indicating the territory controlled by the kingdom of ancient Ghana.

7

This terra-cotta figure was one of many unearthed near the village of Nok, in present-day Nigeria. Created more than 2,000 years ago, the Nok sculptures show that the culture of West Africa was more highly developed than many early European societies.

The professor's opinion was published when the British Empire was at its height, and it represented a point of view that was necessary to justify the continued exploitation of Africans. If, as the professor claimed, Africans had lived in a state of chaos throughout their history, then their European conquerors could believe that they were doing a noble deed by imposing their will and their way of life upon Africa.

The colonialist view of African history held sway into the 20th century. But as the century progressed, more enlightened scholars began to take a fresh look at the African past. As archaeologists (scientists who study the physical remains of past societies) explored the sites of former African cities, they found that Africans had enjoyed a high level of civilization hundreds of years before the arrival of Europeans. In many respects, the kingdoms and cities of Africa had been equal to or more advanced than European societies during the same period.

The kingdom of ancient Ghana, for example, flourished in West Africa at least as early as A.D. 750, when most of Europe was still in the period known as the Dark Ages. In order to fully appreciate Ghana's achievement and the true historical importance of Africa, it is necessary to go back even further in history—millions of years further, to the very origins of the human race.

Chapter 1 | THE CRADLE OF HUMANITY

In 1859, the British biologist Charles Darwin published a book that forever changed the way human beings thought about themselves. Entitled *On the Origin of Species by Means of Natural Selection*, Darwin's book presented a carefully reasoned view of evolution, the process by which all living creatures have changed and developed over millions of years. In a later book, *The Descent of Man* (1871), Darwin addressed the place of human beings in the evolutionary scheme, indicating that modern humans, known by the scientific name *Homo sapiens*, had developed from the basic stock of primates, an order of mammals that includes the apes and monkeys. Darwin's views aroused furious opposition when they were first published; today, after being developed and modified by later scientists, they form the basis of all studies of life on earth.

Among the many groundbreaking ideas Darwin expressed in his books was the conviction that human evolution had begun on the continent of Africa. "In each great region of the world," he wrote, "the living mammals are closely related to the extinct species of the same region. It is, therefore, probable that Africa was formerly inhabited by extinct apes closely allied to the gorilla and chimpanzee; and as these two species are now man's nearest allies, it is somewhat more than probable that our early progenitors lived on the African continent than elsewhere."

Of the 20th-century scholars who have worked to prove Darwin's insight about the importance of Africa, the outstanding figure is Louis S. B. Leakey.

Three Stone Age tools, discovered in Africa during the 1920s. About 2.5 million years ago, human beings inhabiting the continent of Africa began using crude stone implements to skin animals, cut meat, and grind plant foods.

12

Louis S. B. Leakey (1903–72), photographed in Olduvai Gorge, Tanzania, where he and his colleagues made important discoveries of early human remains. As a result of his research, Leakey concluded that modern humans first emerged in Africa about 150,000 years ago.

Born in 1903 to British parents in what is now the East African nation of Kenya, Leakey was educated in England, but he returned to the land of his birth to study the origins of human society. Leakey's greatest work was done in Olduvai Gorge in the nation of Tanzania. Working with his wife, Mary—and later with his sons, Richard and Christopher—Leakey uncovered numerous bones and skull fragments belonging to early hominids, apelike creatures who walked on their hind legs.

The Leakeys' objective was to find enough of these remains, which are known as fossils, to determine how and when the hominids of prehistoric Africa had developed into *Homo sapiens.* After many years of painstaking research, the Leakeys achieved their goal in 1959 and 1960, when they made two major fossil discoveries. Richard Leakey has described them in his book *Origins Reconsidered:* "First was *Zinjanthropus,* a large-toothed, extinct species of hominid. . . . Then there was *Homo habilis* ['handy man']. . . . This was a new species of fossil human—a tool maker, big-brained, a member of our genus, and, according to my father, the direct ancestor of later humans."

The Leakeys' research led them to three main conclusions about Africa's place in history: that the basic stock of primates originated in Africa about 30 to 40 million years ago; that the main branch of human ancestors—the first hominids—developed from the apes 7.5 million years ago; and that *Homo sapiens* emerged in Africa about 150,000 years ago and spread from Africa to the rest of the globe. Though some scholars have argued with the final conclusion, suggesting that *Homo sapiens* may have developed in other regions as well, such as the Middle East, no serious researcher would now think of disputing Africa's crucial role in human history.

Africa provided the right conditions for the development of the human species, but it was not in any way an earthly paradise. Nearly 12 million square miles in area, Africa has always severely chal-

Archaeologists work at a site in Fort Ternan, Kenya, in 1962. By carefully piecing together skull and bone fragments, scientists have been able to shed light on the development of the human species; their findings have confirmed the belief that Africa was the birthplace of humankind.

14

A collection of tools belonging to the Neolithic period, or Late Stone Age. About 10,000 years ago, humans began using tools to plow the earth, enabling them to plant crops: this innovation caused the human population to increase and led to the growth of stable communities.

lenged the creatures occupying its vast expanses. The historian Basil Davidson, in his book *The African Genius,* has provided a vivid description of those challenges:

> There are deserts large enough to swallow half the lands of Europe, where intense heat by day gives way to bitter cold by night, and along whose stony boundaries the grasslands run out and disappear through skylines trembling in a distance eternally flat. There are great forests and

woodlands where the sheer abundance of nature is clearly overwhelming in tall crops of grass that cut like knives, in thorns which catch and hold like hooks of steel, in a myriad marching ants and flies and creeping beasts that bite and itch and nag, in burning heat which sucks and clogs and rains that fall by slow gigantic torrents out of endless skies. . . . There are fine and temperate uplands, tall mountains, rugged hills, but even these are filled with an extravagance of nature.

For several million years, the hominids and early humans who occupied this imposing landscape had no permanent settlements. Instead, they lived as hunter-gatherers. They moved from place to place in groups of no more than 30 individuals, gathering wild plant foods, hunting animals where they could, and sometimes feeding on carcasses left behind by lions and hyenas. When the plants in a region were exhausted or the animals moved to new habitats, the ancestors of humanity moved on as well. The tools they first began to use about 2.5 million years ago were simple devices fashioned from stones—thus the earliest period of human history is known as the Stone Age.

About 10,000 years ago, human beings developed the ability to use their stone implements to plow the earth. This enabled them to plant seeds and raise crops that provided them with food. Now humans were able to create permanent settlements near their fields. In this setting, they could also build defenses against wild animals and other humans; and with a comparatively large food supply available, the human population was able to increase dramatically.

A major change occurred in the life of these growing communities about 2,500 years ago. At that time, human beings discovered how to extract iron ore from the earth: when heated in a fire, the iron could be shaped into tools and weapons. The coming of the Iron Age quickly changed the way people lived. Iron implements were much sharper and stronger than those made of stone and bone. With iron plows and iron axes, humans could clear and cultivate areas that had previously been unsuitable for farming. By about 2,000 years ago, all the potentially fertile regions of the African continent were settled by the ancestors of modern-day Africans—though the total population of 3 to 4 million was a far cry from the 485 million of the late 20th century.

In Africa's new order, groups that possessed iron-tipped spears and arrows were better able to protect their communities, and they were also able to conquer peoples armed with more primitive weapons. It was only a matter of time, therefore, until the Iron Age gave birth to kingdoms and empires on the continent of Africa.

Chapter 2 | ACROSS THE SAHARA

A Stone Age rock engraving of a bull, discovered in North Africa, one of the first regions of the continent to achieve prosperity. After the introduction of the camel during the 4th century A.D., North African merchants began to make regular trips across the Sahara Desert in order to trade with West Africans.

Between 10,000 B.C. and 3,000 B.C., the Sahara, which lies between North and West Africa, was a fertile area that was home to both cattle raisers and farmers. By the 5th century B.C., however, the Greek historian Herodotus was obliged to describe the Sahara in the following terms: "Beyond the ridge southwards [from Libya in North Africa], in the direction of the interior, the country is a desert, with no springs, no beasts, no rain, no wood, and altogether destitute of moisture." The dramatic change in the Sahara had two important effects: it forced the herders and farmers on the Sahara's southern edges to move farther south, and it imposed a formidable barrier between the interior and the rest of the world. As a result, West Africa did not develop as quickly as neighboring regions

to the east and the south. Egypt and North Africa, by contrast, benefited greatly from their location on the Mediterranean Sea: close contact with peoples such as the Phoenicians, Greeks, and Romans made North Africa and Egypt highly prosperous by the 4th century B.C.

Nevertheless, West Africa did develop—at its own pace and in its own style. South of the Sahara and extending all the way from the Atlantic Ocean to the Gulf of Aden in the Middle East was a vast plain commonly referred to as the African savanna. Though the savanna contained many different environments—some dry and open, some moist and wooded—it was, until it merged with the dense tropical rain forests along the Atlantic coast, an area that was both friendly to human settlement and rela-

18

tively easy to travel through. As the archaeologist Graham Connah has pointed out in his 1987 book *African Civilizations,* the region's diversity aided its growth: "Each environment possessed some resources but lacked others. . . . The complexity of the West African environment, as a whole, provided conditions conducive to the development of a complex network of regional trade. . . . It is quite likely that such trading activity was almost as old as West African food production and the development of a trading network could well have been already in existence by about three thousand years ago."

Connah's suggestion fits well with the testimony of Herodotus, who reported that the Carthaginians, residents of a wealthy city in what is now Tunisia, had sailed part of the way down the western coast in order to trade with the inhabitants of the interior. Later writers stated that the Romans, whose civilization flourished from the 4th century B.C. into the Christian era, had acquired through the Garamantes of Libya many wild animals from the interior of Africa to supply their circuses and gladiatorial shows. Ancient rock paintings found in North Africa, on the edges of the Sahara, depict horses and chariots; they indicate that long-established chariot routes ran from north to south long before any written record was made of contacts between the peoples of the coast and those of the mysterious interior.

For several centuries, these contacts were limited by the nature of the Sahara itself. More than 3 million square miles in area, the Sahara is the world's largest desert. Because temperatures during the day can reach as high as 120 degrees Fahrenheit and supplies of water are scant, the 40-day journey across the desert required courage, determination, and careful planning. Travelers who became separated from their companions were seldom seen again. The trans-Sahara trek became somewhat easier after the 4th century A.D., when camels were introduced in place of horses; camels are able to travel long distances without water, and their wider hooves make it easier for them to move through sand. However, intensive contact between North Africa and the interior did not begin until the 7th century, when a revolutionary change took place in the political and religious life of the region. By this time, the old empires of the Mediterranean and the Middle East were in decline or in ruins. In their place was a powerful new force—Islam.

The religion of Islam arose in the deserts of Arabia, to the east of Africa. The inhabitants of Arabia, who were mainly farmers and wandering herders, had for centuries worshiped a variety of gods and spirits, many of them associated with forces of nature. In this form of worship, the Arabians were following the earliest inhabitants of the Middle East, peoples such as the Sumerians and Assyrians, who had created the world's first great civilizations. As they honored these age-old beliefs, however, the Arabians were in close contact with peoples who practiced more recent religions, such as Judaism and Christianity. Both Judaism and Christianity were based upon worship of a single god. Both religions had been founded by powerful figures who had experienced what they believed to be a direct communication from God, revealing a great truth for all humanity.

The prophet who emerged to express a new religious idea in Arabia was named Muhammad. Born in the city of Mecca in 570 A.D., Muhammad spent his youth as a camel driver and then became a tradesman. At the age of 40, he had a vision of a new religion based on the worship of a single god, Allah, who demanded strict devotion, regular prayer, and pure habits in return for eternal salvation. Muham-

A Persian miniature depicts the arrival of Muhammad in Medina in 622, after his flight from Mecca. By the time of his death 10 years later, the Prophet had attracted masses of followers. His teachings formed the basis of Islam, one of the world's great religions.

19

mad quickly attracted a group of followers, but he also aroused bitter opposition among the Arabian tribespeople, who felt that he was attacking their traditional beliefs and way of life. In 622, Muhammad's enemies forced him to leave Mecca and resettle in Medina. There he continued to gather converts, who became known as Muslims, and to develop the principles that grew into the religion of Islam. By the time of Muhammad's death in 632, his influence had spread throughout Arabia; his teaching was recorded in the holy book known as the Koran, which has the same importance for Muslims that the Old Testament has for Jews and the New Testament has for Christians.

According to the historian Albert Hourani, Muhammad expressed his final message to his followers in a speech he made in Mecca just before his death: "Fighting between [Muslims] should be avoided, and the blood shed in pagan times should not be avenged; Muslims should fight all men until they say, 'There is no God but God.' "

In practice, Muhammad's followers modified these instructions. Because they considered both Jews and Christians "peoples of the Book" who had received earlier versions of the message received in final form by Muhammad, Muslims made no attempt to convert either group to Islam. But all those peoples, Arabs and non-Arabs, who still followed pagan religions were ripe for conversion, either by argument or by force. Even here, according to the Moroccan scholar M. El Fasi, the Muslims were not overly aggressive; they sanctioned war "if certain conditions were fulfilled, such as the fact that the unbelievers should be the first to commence hostilities and that there should be a reasonable hope of success."

Muhammad's followers, led by his father-in-law Abu Bakr, applied these doctrines with great success: by 645, Muslim warriors had conquered all of Arabia and much of the Middle East. From there they moved westward into the central part of North Africa, known as the Maghrib. By the end of the 7th century, the Muslims had extended their power to the Atlantic coast of Africa, and shortly afterward they crossed the Strait of Gibraltar to conquer much of present-day Spain and Portugal.

Throughout the territories they conquered, the Muslims created a highly sophisticated culture that emphasized religious observance, art, architecture, learning, and commerce. Intellectually and physically, the Muslims were a restless, energetic group, always eager to push forward into unknown regions. Not surprisingly, Muslim scholars and traders soon turned their attention to the area their geographers called Bilad al-

20

Sudan, Arabic for "the land of the black peoples."

The title bestowed on West Africa by the Muslim geographers is significant. During the 19th century, some Europeans put forth the theory that all the kingdoms and cities of West Africa had been founded by a race of light-skinned North Africans called Hamites, and that the darker-skinned Africans had always been the subjects of the Hamites, never creating great civilizations of their own. Later scholars discarded this notion, pointing out that the term *Hamitic* pertains only to a group of languages and has nothing to do with race. Modern anthropologists such as Richard Leakey also reject the idea that there is any connection between a people's skin color and its capacity for achievement and self-government. Differences in pigmentation, scientists now recognize, are based solely upon climate and have nothing to do with intellectual ability. When human beings lived exclusively in the torrid regions of Africa, they were all dark skinned because dark pigmentation protected them from the harmful ultraviolet rays of the sun, which can cause skin cancer and other diseases. As *Homo sapiens* migrated from Africa to colder climates where there was far less sunlight, heavy

21

The Great Mosque of Kairouan, in present-day Tunisia, dates from the 7th century. The first major Islamic house of worship in North Africa, the building and its vast courtyard reflect the artistry and skill of Muslim architects.

pigmentation became a drawback—it prevented the skin from absorbing the amount of sunlight needed to produce vitamin D, which is essential for the growth of bones and teeth. Hence lighter skin began to predominate in Europe, with the peoples of the Mediterranean, the Middle East, and North Africa occupying a middle ground between light-skinned Europeans and dark-skinned Africans.

While Greek, Phoenician, Roman, and Arab influences were creating a rich and varied society in North Africa, the

22

These terra-cotta sculptures from Nok are among the treasures of world art. Scholars believe that most of the figures represent important ancestors and that they were made for display in family shrines.

Sudan was producing a remarkable culture centered on the village of Nok in what is now central Nigeria. The modern world was generally ignorant of the Nok culture until the 1930s, when tin-mining operations near the village uncovered numerous small sculptures, mostly of human faces. The pieces were modeled in terra-cotta, a form of clay that can be heated to a lasting hardness. Possibly created as early as 400 B.C.—in other words, at least as early as the acclaimed pottery and sculpture of ancient Greece—the Nok figurines greatly impressed art experts. As Basil Davidson has written in his book *Africa in History,* "These figures are remarkable for their great artistic qualities, combining . . . a rare sensitivity to human character and features with a sophistication of style that seems extraordinary for the times in which they were made." While Nok was flourishing, the barbarian tribes of western Europe, whose descendants would eventually colonize Africa, produced virtually no art of any kind.

The Muslims of North Africa, for their part, had no idea of belonging to a "superior" Hamitic race. They believed that their religion surpassed all others, but their religion stressed the equality of all Muslims before Allah. Guided by intellectual curiosity and a desire to prosper through trade, they had a clear view of the identity and achievements of the peoples they were contacting south of the Sahara. The most prominent of these groups was the Soninke, who lived in the northernmost part of the Sudan, bordering on the Sahara. With the stimulus of Muslim contacts, the Soninke were able to create the first great black kingdom of the Sudan.

23

Chapter 3 | WAGADU

West African peoples such as the Soninke did not keep written records of their history. Instead they relied upon stories passed from generation to generation by storytellers, often known as *griots*. Scholars refer to this method of recounting history with the term *oral tradition*, and during the 20th century they have recognized that the oral traditions of Africa are remarkably accurate. Even in cases where oral tradition does not describe exact events, it tells a great deal about the culture of a people. The oral traditions of the Soninke, for example, are heavily influenced by their religious beliefs. They also show that the Soninke were well established in the Sudan long before they felt the influence of North African Muslims.

The Soninke, who are still flourishing in various regions of West Africa, have given modern scholars several different accounts of their distant past. Though they vary in detail, all the Soninke traditions center about the figure of Dinga, who came to Africa from the East, married, and sired children who founded various kingdoms in the region. Dinga's son Dyabe, for example, founded a kingdom at the town of Kumbi (later Kumbi Saleh, the capital of ancient Ghana) and divided his realm into four provinces, each ruled by a warrior chief who had come to Dyabe's support upon hearing him beat a sacred drum known as the *tabala*. The descendants of Dyabe and the four chiefs became known as the *wago*, the ruling elite of the Soninke. For

Travelers cross the Sahel, the semiarid region between the Sahara and the Sudan. During Ghana's heyday, the arduous trans-Sahara journey took a full two months; even experienced travelers were liable to lose their way in the shifting sands of the desert and perish from lack of water.

this reason the Soninke called their first kingdom Wagadu.

Wagadu flourished under the rule of seven successive kings. According to tradition, though, the founding of Wagadu had resulted from an agreement between Dyabe and Bida, a great black snake who guarded Kumbi. Bida allowed the Soninke to settle in Kumbi only on condition that the Soninke sacrifice a beautiful young woman in his honor every year. The Soninke carried out this obligation faithfully for many years, but one year a young man who was in love with the woman offered for sacrifice rushed forward and killed the snake. As a result, Bida's curse fell upon the Soninke. The rain that had watered their crops ceased to fall for seven years, and many of the Soninke were forced to scatter throughout the Sudan in search of more fertile land.

There is no reason to doubt that the Soninke's oral traditions recount an actual chain of events: the founding of an ancient state (at least as early as 500 A.D.) and its sudden decline due to a prolonged drought, similar to the more recent drought that afflicted the Sudan during the 1970s. The value of the account is in no way diminished by details, such as the magic drum and the vengeful snake, that would not be accepted as historical truth by scholars. Those who have studied African culture understand that the mythical elements in the Soninke tradition, and others like it, are not mere fantasies cooked up by storytellers. They represent important beliefs shared by many Africans, both in ancient times and today, and they reveal much about Africans' attitudes toward their land and their history.

As Basil Davidson has pointed out, one of the main principles cherished by Africans—who had struggled to make a place for themselves in a large and often punishing continent—was the harmony of human beings with their environment. In most African religions, various animals and forces of nature are endowed with spiritual power, the snake being among the creatures most often regarded as sacred. Many African religious ceremonies are directed toward appeasing the spirits of the skies, earth, and waters; through these rituals, the worshipers hope to ensure that the rain will fall, the crops will grow, and the rivers will teem with fish. For the Soninke, there could be no greater symbol of their claim to hold the territory around Kumbi than the belief that their presence had been accepted by a creature representing the power of the earth. And in order to cope

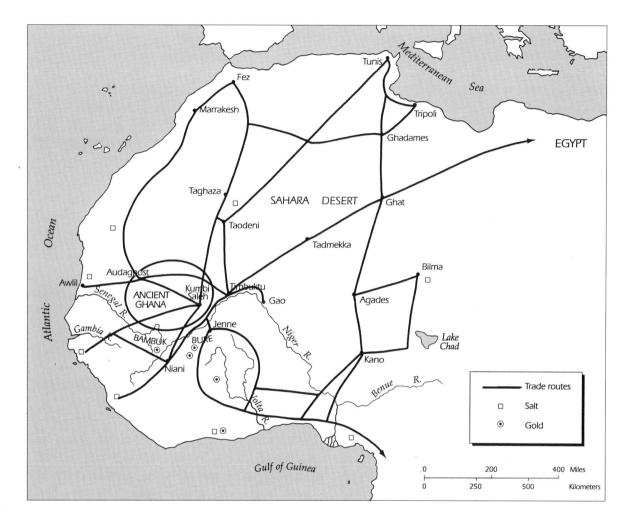

A map of West Africa showing the major gold- and salt-producing regions. The Soninke state, founded on the site of Kumbi Saleh, eventually grew rich because of its proximity to the Bambuk goldfields.

27

with the unpredictable forces of nature that could threaten their very existence, it was valuable for the Soninke to believe that they could influence their destiny through proper thought and action.

Apart from their ability to grow crops, the single most important influence on the future of the Soninke was the presence of gold in West Africa. It was this precious metal that made the Sudan so alluring to the North Africans and made the dangerous trek across the Sahara worthwhile. Like the Romans and the Carthaginians before them, the Muslims of Egypt and North Africa based their monetary system on gold coins, the most common being the *dinar*, which was equal in value to an eighth of an ounce of gold. During Roman times, central Europe had provided a steady source of gold for coinage. By the time the Muslims gained control of North Africa, however, the gold mines of Europe had been exhausted. Muslim rulers realized that controlling access to the Sudan's gold—and thus the entire world's currency supply—could bring them vast wealth and great power.

There is no record of the exact techniques used by Africans to extract gold, because they never allowed outsiders to see the mines. However, it is likely that the mining process was carried out much as it had been years earlier by the Greeks and Romans. These people did leave some records of their operations, which have been summarized by J. G. Landels in *Engineering in the Ancient World:* "In mining operations [the use of animal power, common in later times] seems to have been almost negligible, for obvious practical reasons. Unless there was ac-

cess via horizontal tunnels ('adits') it would be very difficult indeed to get animals in and out of a mine, and ancient workings did not normally include entrance adits or any galleries or spaces in which animals could be kept, fed and housed underground. The haulage of ores and spoil seems to have been done exclusively by man-power, using buckets on ropes, and it was extracted via the nearest shaft, not taken along any great distance underground."

This was a laborious procedure, especially compared with modern methods employing mechanical drills and motorized trams for removal of ore and slag; in order to extract large amounts of gold, the Africans clearly had to achieve a high degree of discipline and organization. In the third volume of the *UNESCO General History of Africa*, the French scholar J. Devisse estimates that West Africans exported between two and three tons of gold a year and mined an equal amount for their own use. Devisse further calculates that each shaft yielded between 2.5 and 5 grams of gold, that is, not much more than the amount required to mint a single dinar. "Between 240,000 and 480,000 shafts thus needed to be dug each year," Devisse writes, "which represents a considerable mobilization of labor. Even if we add on the output from gold-washing [panning for gold in streams] the fact remains that this activity . . . must have mobilized hundreds of thousands of people in West Africa each year once the demand was strong and regular."

Because of the Muslims' spectacular success as warriors, their first impulse was simply to seize gold from the Sudan by force. Arabic sources indicate that tribesmen from the Sahara raided the Sudan in 734, securing a large supply of gold as well as a number of captives who were employed as slaves by the North Africans. However, the Arab governors soon realized that periodic raids could not secure a continuous flow of gold. Since the Muslims possessed camels for the trans-Sahara journey, they pursued the more stable course of establishing regular trade relations with the Africans of the Sudan.

In order to trade, of course, the Muslims had to supply some need on the part of the Sudanese. The major commodity they had to offer was salt. Owing in large part to the drying out of the Sahara, North Africa possessed a number of naturally occurring salt deposits, and the peoples of the region had been mining salt for several centuries. Below the Sahara, however, salt was in short supply, obtainable only from seawater that collected at the mouths of rivers in the forest belt.

Those Africans in the Sudan who ate the meat of wild animals were able to obtain a sufficient supply of salt. But those who lived mainly on freshwater fish and plant foods such as sorghum and millet found it difficult to keep up their salt intake. They learned by harsh experience that salt is not merely a substance that adds flavor to foods; a daily intake of salt is required to maintain the body's water balance and muscle function, especially in hot climates, where active people quickly lose salt and other essential minerals (such as potassium) through perspiration. Thus the Africans of the Sudan were more than willing to trade their precious gold for what is now, in many parts of the world, a common household item. Once this commerce was established, the Soninke emerged from their period of decline and became a powerful nation.

29

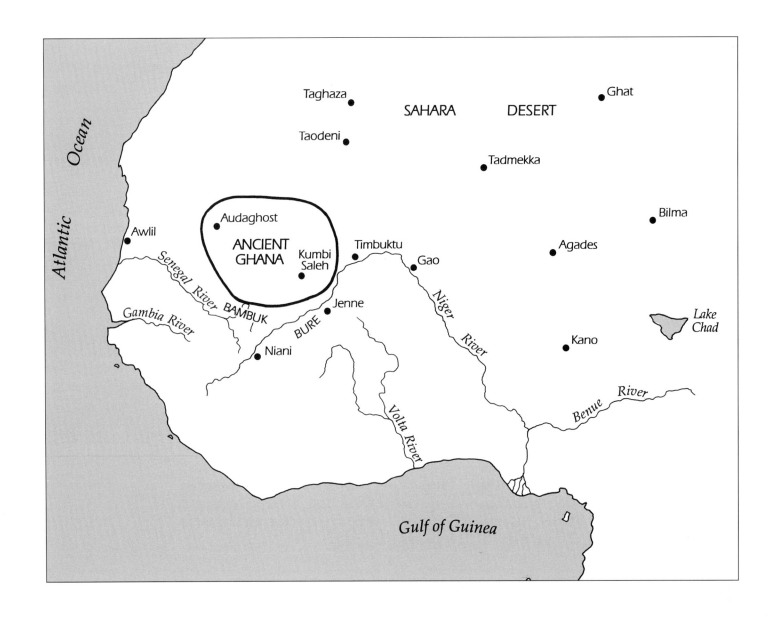

Chapter 4 | THE LAND OF GOLD

At its height, ancient Ghana comprised a substantial territory between the Senegal and Niger rivers. By uniting their ancestral communities into a centralized kingdom, the Soninke people changed the course of West African history.

Wagadu, the Soninke's original state, had been relatively small, and it was reduced still further after the migration caused by the seven-year drought. Eventually, the new Soninke trading empire came to occupy a large area that lay between the Senegal River and the western branch of the Niger River. As the kingdom grew, it became known throughout Africa as Ghana.

The term *ghana*, which means "war chief" in the Mande language, was originally used just to describe one of the functions of the Soninke kings. Gradually, no doubt owing to the importance of military power in Soninke expansion, the new term came to serve as the name of the state itself.

A second title held by the king of Ghana was *kaya-magha*, or "master of the gold." (Some Arabic chronicles refer to the Soninke kingdom as Kaya-Magha.) Thus the king's two most important functions were leadership in war and control of the gold trade. The dual role played by their kings helped the Soninke become the first people of the Sudan to develop a powerful centralized state and a strong tradition of kingship, both of which were to play an important role in later West African history.

Before the rise of ancient Ghana, African society had been based on clans, or descent lines. People who shared a common ancestor lived in extended communities and managed their own affairs, with the eldest members of the clan having the most authority. Most often, members of a given clan were not allowed to marry within the clan; young men were required to journey forth to find a mate from a neighboring clan. In this way, ties were formed between different descent lines.

In theory, all descent lines had equal standing. When decisions had to be made regarding the people as a whole, the heads of descent lines would meet and deliberate. In practice, however, it may be assumed that the heads of the most populous descent lines often gained greater influence in the councils of their peoples. This was quite possibly the case with Dinga, the founder of Wagadu, even though Soninke tradition tended to justify his rule through accounts of his power to make peace with the forces of nature.

As the Soninke gained influence as traders and expanded their territory, the advantage of having a single leader surely became obvious to them. In order to control neighboring peoples and ensure safety for trading caravans, it was desirable for the Soninke to employ unified military forces under a central command. When dealing with trading partners, there was much advantage to be gained from having a single spokesman who could express a definite policy and guarantee that agreements would be carried out.

The power of Ghana ultimately rested on the Soninke's superior skill in working iron. Iron smelting in West Africa dated back to A.D. 500, coinciding with the founding of the first Soninke state. Because of iron's importance, blacksmiths were often reputed to have magical powers; in some communities, they lived apart from the rest of the populace, as people both respected and feared them. Over the centuries, the techniques they used appear to have changed very little. When Mungo Park visited West Africa at the end of the 18th century, he was allowed to see a smelting furnace in operation in Kamalia, a village near the Niger River. His description of the device tallies with archaeologists' sketches of furnaces in operation hundreds of years earlier.

According to Park, the furnace consisted of a circular clay tower, 10 feet high and 3 feet in diameter. The tower was reinforced with slender branches to prevent the clay from cracking under the intense heat of the smelting process. Around the bottom of the furnace the smiths had made seven holes. Into each hole they fitted a clay tube: by sealing or opening the ends of the tubes they could regulate the flow of air into the furnace and control the intensity of the fire. Park described the actual smelting in the following terms:

(Continued on page 37)

32

ANCIENT AFRICAN ART

Little was known about the ancient people of West Africa before the 20th century, when examples of stunning artwork were discovered. Rock paintings found in the Sahara date back as far as 8000 B.C. and tell much about the economic activities and religious beliefs of the people who made them. Terra-cotta figures found by miners in northern Nigeria in the 1930s are the oldest known examples of West African sculpture. They were created by the Nok culture, which flourished between 500 B.C. and A.D. 200.

This rock painting in Oran, Algeria, was left by Berbers traveling through the Sahara around 100 B.C. Before camels were introduced to western Africa in the 4th century A.D., traders relied on horses to transport their goods across the expansive desert.

Terra-cotta elephant head from Nok.

Terra-cotta head from Nok.

Terra-cotta head from Nok.

(Continued from page 32)

The iron-stone which I saw was very heavy, of a dull red color, with grayish specks; it was broken into pieces about the size of a hen's egg. A bundle of dry wood was first put into the furnace, and covered with a considerable quantity of charcoal, which was brought, ready burnt, from the woods. Over this was laid a stratum of iron-stone, and then another of charcoal, and so on, until the furnace was quite full. The fire was applied through one of the tubes, and blown for some time with bellows made of goats' skins. . . . On the second night, some of the tubes were withdrawn, and the air allowed to have freer access to the furnace; but the heat was still very great, and a bluish flame rose some feet above the top of the furnace. On the third day . . . all the tubes were taken out, the ends of many of them being vitrified by the heat; but the metal was not removed until some days afterwards, when the whole was perfectly cool. Part of the furnace was then taken down, and the iron appeared in the form of a large irregular mass, with pieces of charcoal adhering to it. . . . This iron, or rather steel, is formed into various instruments, by being repeatedly heated in a forge. . . The hammer, forceps, and anvil, are all very simple, and the workmanship (particularly in the formation of knives and spears) is not destitute of merit. The iron, indeed, is hard and brittle; and requires much labor before it can be made to answer the purpose.

Equipped with iron-tipped spears and arrows, Ghana's armies were able to subdue the forces of their West African neighbors, most of whom fought with weapons made of stone, bone, and wood. As for the gold so eagerly sought by the Muslim traders, Ghana itself actually possessed none. The precious metal was mined at Bambuk, which lies between the Senegal and Faleme rivers, just to the south of Ghana's territory. Given Ghana's military might, Bambuk must have presented a tempting target for conquest. However, the goldfields were located in the forest belt, and the people of Bambuk took great pains to keep the location of the mines a secret from outsiders. According to Nehemiah Levtzion, the gold producers still engaged in the "silent trade" described by Herodotus several centuries earlier:

> Traders coming from the north laid down their goods on the bank of a river and withdrew. Then came people with gold, laid some of it against each pile of goods and retreated. When given the sign the traders came forward, and if satisfied by the amount of gold left, they took it; otherwise they withdrew again and waited for

Camels laden with slabs of salt from the Sahara wend their way into the Sudan. Salt was such a precious commodity in the torrid climate of West Africa that the Sudanese often used chunks of salt in place of money.

38

the local people to add more gold. As soon as the traders disappeared with the gold, the local buyers collected the goods they had bought.

In order to reach the goldfields, the traders had to pass through Ghana's territory, and the Soninke thus became a crucial link in the trading process, exact-

ing payment from both parties to every transaction. For each load of salt that entered Ghana from the north, the king collected an import tax of one dinar. For each load of salt that left Ghana for the south, the king collected an export tax of two dinars from Ghana's southern neighbors, the gold producers. (As distance from the Sahara increased, salt became scarcer and hence more valuable.) In this manner, Ghana became known throughout the world as the Land of Gold, without ever producing an ounce of the precious metal.

The Soninke also carefully regulated the flow of gold across their borders, making sure that the metal would not become so widely available that its value would drop. During the 9th and 10th centuries, when various factions in the Muslim world began to compete for power, Ghana's monopoly on the gold trade became extremely lucrative. As both the Umayyad and Fatimid dynasties challenge rose to the ruling Abbasids, these groups asserted their independence by minting their own gold coins for all transactions. Their only source of high-quality gold was Ghana, and as a result traders from all corners of the Muslim world began to converge on the Sudanese kingdom.

Chapter 5 | THE NEW SOCIETY

Archaeologists constructed this model of the Great Mosque of Kumbi Saleh, which was unearthed during the early 20th century. At the height of its splendor, the capital of ancient Ghana was home to more than 30,000 people.

As the wealth of Ghana increased, the Soninke kings strove to live up to their growing importance, and they maintained their kingdom at a level of grandeur that deeply impressed traders and other visitors. The most reliable accounts of Ghana were compiled during the 11th century by al-Bakri, an Arab writer living in the Spanish city of Córdoba, which was then under Muslim control. In al-Bakri's day, Ghana's ruler was Tunka Manin, who, according to al-Bakri, could "put two hundred thousand warriors in the field, more than forty thousand of them being armed with bow and arrow." Most likely, this figure is somewhat inflated; but in order to maintain the safety of trade routes throughout his territory and discourage raiders from the north, Tunka Manin would certainly

have needed a large and intimidating military force—and he would have made sure that visitors were aware of its power. No less impressive to al-Bakri's informants was the splendor of the royal court:

> When [the king] gives an audience to his people, to listen to their complaints and set them to rights, he sits in a pavilion around which stand his horses caparisoned in cloth of gold; behind him stand ten pages holding shields and gold-mounted swords; and on his right are the sons of the princes of his empire, splendidly clad and with gold plaited into their hair. The governor of the city is seated on the ground next to the king, and all around him are his counsellors in the same position. The gate of the chamber is guarded by dogs of an excellent breed. These dogs never leave the

king's seat. They wear collars of gold and silver, ornamented with metals.

Other travelers reported, perhaps a bit more fancifully, that Tunka Manin held enormous banquets attended by thousands of guests and that he possessed a nugget of gold so large that he could tether his horse to it.

It seems likely that the capital city moved several times during Ghana's history. Arab writers often referred to both the kingdom and the capital as Ghana. But scholars are increasingly confident that at the time of al-Bakri's accounts, the capital was Kumbi Saleh, the original center of Wagadu. Archaeologists first uncovered the ruins of Kumbi Saleh in 1914; during the following decades, researchers working at the site reconstructed the outlines of a large city, whose population may have reached as high as 30,000. Kumbi Saleh actually consisted of two settlements, one for the West Africans and the other for visiting Muslim traders—a pattern that would be followed by other great trading centers in the Sudan.

In the Soninke town, the houses were built in the typical West African manner, with circular walls of clay and cone-shaped thatched roofs. In the Muslim quarter, the style of building followed the architecture of such great Muslim cities as Cairo, Baghdad, and Damascus. The houses were rectangular and made of stone, most of them having two stories and some containing as many as nine rooms. Typically, the bottom floor was used by the traders for storing their goods, and the top floor served as a residence. As Richard W. Hull points out in his book *African Cities and Towns Before the European Conquest,* the Muslim style gradually influenced the way the Sudanese constructed their buildings. By the 13th and 14th centuries, West African architecture came to exhibit a wide variety of forms and techniques.

Though later West African monarchs often converted to Islam in order to gain the confidence of the Muslim traders, the kings of Ghana apparently felt no such necessity. Kings such as Tunka Manin were more concerned with maintaining their status among their own people. Because Ghana was the first of the centralized kingdoms, the elevation of the king above the leaders of other descent lines would have been an especially sensitive issue. In order to maintain his right to exercise leadership and command obedience, the king needed to convince his subjects that he was the supreme guardian of all the traditions and religious beliefs of the Soninke. According to al-Bakri, the king maintained a rather menacing air of religious mystery around his private compound, which was surrounded by a protective wall: "Around the king's town are domed huts and groves where live the sorcerers, the men in charge of [the Soninke's] religious cult. In these are also the idols and the tombs of their kings. These groves are guarded, no one can enter them nor discover their contents. The prisons of the king are there, and if anyone is imprisoned in them, no more is ever heard of him."

Other visitors described the personal status cultivated by the king. He and his eldest son were the only Ghanaians allowed to wear sewn clothing in the Muslim style, and whenever the king appeared, his subjects were required to fall on the ground and throw dust on their heads. The visiting Muslims were not expected to show such extreme deference: they greeted the king simply by clapping their hands.

Even the tombs of the kings, and the rituals associated with them, were calculated to create awe in the minds of Ghana's people. In recent years, archaeologists have discovered a number of burial mounds, also known as tumuli, in the West African savanna. The mounds

43

were carefully and sturdily constructed of various materials, including wood, stone, earth, and clay. Several date from the era when ancient Ghana flourished, and their remains substantiate the account of royal burial practices given by al-Bakri:

> When the king dies, they build a huge dome of wood over the burial place. Then they bring him on a bed lightly covered, and put him inside the dome. At his side they place his orna-

A Muslim school during the Middle Ages. Although Islam exerted a strong cultural influence in West Africa, the majority of West Africans continued to follow their traditional religions, which center upon the spiritual forces at work in nature.

44

ments, his arms, and the vessels from which he used to eat and drink, filled with food and beverages. They bring in those men who used to serve his food and drink. Then they close the door of the dome and cover it with mats and other materials. People gather and pile earth over it until it becomes like a large mound. Then they dig a ditch around it so that it can be reached only from one place. They sacrifice to their dead and make offerings of intoxicating drinks.

The upkeep of a city such as Kumbi Saleh, not to mention a kingdom of Ghana's size, required political organization as well as wealth and intimidation. For this reason, the king was obliged to appoint a series of governors, who were charged with safeguarding the trade routes through their provinces and with collecting the king's taxes. The governors had a wide range of powers, but they were ultimately servants of the king, and all of them paid tribute to the central government. As the governors were the heads of leading descent lines, uncertainty about their loyalty to the king must always have been a cause of concern. Al-Bakri, in his description of the royal court, noted that the sons of the "princes of [the king's] empire" sat with the king. On one hand, the presence of the governors' sons in Kumbi Saleh was

a mark of royal favor; on the other hand, it was a way of ensuring that the boys' fathers would not be tempted to serve their own interests rather than the king's.

Ghana's system of interlocking governments was the foundation of the empire's wealth and stability. As Basil Davidson and F. K. Buah have written in their *History of West Africa,* "The growth and conduct of trade over a wide region meant peace and security over this region; and many people of Ghana benefited from this. The formation of Ghana and its growth into a large empire therefore marked an important stage in social development. It was a big political and economic achievement." Davidson and Buah also point out that by regulating the flow of gold to keep the price high, the kings of Ghana were pioneers in sophisticated economic techniques:

> Ancient Ghana, in short, adopted the monopoly system that is employed to this day for another precious commodity, diamonds. Most of the diamonds of the world are mined by a handful of big companies. These companies . . . have agreed among themselves not to put all the diamonds they mine on the market. If they did, they would drive down the price, for diamonds would then cease to be

(Continued on page 49)

KUMBI SALEH

The ruins of Kumbi Saleh reveal the impressive size and prosperity of the capital of ancient Ghana. The photos on these pages, taken during Professor Jean Devisse's excavations in 1987, show the section of the city inhabited by Muslim traders. In building their houses and mosques, the Muslims retained their own architectural style, creating neighborhoods that differed radically from those of the native Ghanaians.

The Great Mosque of Kumbi Saleh.

46

A house dating from the 13th or 14th century. Below this structure are the remains of older buildings, which indicate that the site was inhabited as early as the 7th century.

A triangular niche adorns the entrance of a house in Kumbi Saleh.

(Continued from page 44)

scarce; and what is not scarce is not expensive. Instead, the diamond companies sell their diamonds in small quantities . . . so their price stays high. The old emperors of Ghana did much the same with their pieces or nuggets of gold.

By developing political and economic practices never before experienced in West Africa, the kings of Ghana placed their empire on a par—at the very least—with any state of medieval Europe. There are striking parallels between Ghana's Tunka Manin and William the Conqueror, the French nobleman who seized control of England in 1066 and crowned himself King William I. Under the feudal system of government practiced by William, lords and vassals were bound together by ties of mutual loyalty. Vassals—in this case, the barons of England—held their territories by grant from King William; in return, they paid him taxes and pledged their support in time of war. No baron had the right to wage war on his own, and all were compelled by various legal traditions to pledge their obedience to the king. The same principles prevailed in Ghana, only on a much grander scale. William had invaded England with only 5,000 men-at-arms, and his swift victory over the nation's Anglo-Saxon rulers was due as much to

A West African griot playing the kora, *a traditional West African instrument. In addition to performing as traveling musicians, many griots in modern Africa recite oral traditions that have been passed down over the course of centuries. Scholars have found these verbal chronicles remarkably accurate in their portrayal of the African past.*

49

England's poverty and disarray as to William's own strength. He would certainly have envied the vast army at the command of Tunka Manin, not to mention the wealth and splendor of Kumbi Saleh.

Chapter 6 | MENACE FROM THE NORTH

North African troops in battle, as depicted in a medieval Spanish manuscript. When Almoravid forces from North Africa captured Kumbi Saleh in 1076, the kingdom of ancient Ghana suffered a blow from which it never fully recovered.

Ghana may have enjoyed a monopoly over the gold trade, but it had no monopoly on the idea of expansion, which had been the common property of many nations and peoples. For the better part of three centuries, Ghana had possessed enough military power to discourage any neighbors with dreams of conquest. By the 11th century, however, a new group—the Almoravids—arose to challenge the established political and cultural order throughout the Sudan and the Maghrib. Eventually, Ghana would become their victim.

The Almoravids were, from the standpoint of the 11th century, newcomers in the Muslim world. They owed their origin to a Muslim teacher named Abd Allah Ibn Yasin, who had traveled from Arabia into the Sahara around 1039. Ibn Yasin had been summoned by a tribal leader who wished his people to have religious instruction. As it happened, Ibn Yasin practiced a very strict form of Islam that allowed very little in the way of personal enjoyment. This approach to religion had little in common with the general tone of Muslim society in the 11th century, especially the graceful and prosperous societies of North Africa and Spain. When Ibn Yasin's sponsor died, therefore, his unhappy pupils took the opportunity to drive him away.

Ibn Yasin was not discouraged. He traveled to the Atlantic coast, where he founded a fortified religious community known as a *ribat*. He had great success in attracting followers, who became known in Arabic as *al-Murabitun*, "the people of the ribat," from which the name Al-

52

moravid was eventually derived. When he had gathered sufficient forces, Ibn Yasin conquered the Saharans who had once rejected him and made himself master of the northern desert. In 1054, the Almoravids sacked Awdaghust, the northernmost of Ghana's major cities, but did not press farther into Ghana's domains. Following Ibn Yasin's death in battle in 1059, the Almoravids split into two groups. The northern group, under Yusuf Ibn Tashfin, systematically took control of North Africa and then swept into al-Andalus (the Muslim territories of Spain) with the object of displacing the established Muslim rulers. The southern group, led by Abu Bakr, set its sights on Ghana.

Abu Bakr began his campaign against Ghana in 1070 by forming an alliance with the people of Takrur, a kingdom on Africa's Atlantic coast. However, Ghana's armies were so powerful that Abu Bakr's forces were unable to capture Kumbi Saleh until 1076. By contrast, the Almoravid forces that invaded Spain during the next decade made short work of a supposedly invincible Christian army at the Battle of Sagrajas in 1086. They seemed certain to conquer all of Spain until the Spanish knight Rodrigo Díaz, the legendary El Cid, defeated them at the Battle of Cuarte in 1094 and permanently stemmed the tide of their advance.

The Muslim leaders of earlier centuries had never attempted to convert the Sudanese to Islam, but the Almoravids had always been a more militant group. They lost no time in imposing their religion on Ghana. The Almoravids also employed Ghanaian troops in a war against the neighboring city of Tadmekka in 1085, one of the aims of this war being to convert the Tadmekkans to Islam.

However, the Almoravids eventually grew to understand the wisdom of earlier Muslim leaders, who had concluded that it would be no easy matter to hold Ghana by force. As quoted by Nehemiah Levtzion, the great 14th-century Arab historian Ibn Khaldun described the eventual fate of the Almoravid conquerors: "Those of them who had founded an empire in Morocco and Spain were lost. . . . They were consumed by the exercise of authority, swallowed up in the vast territories, destroyed by luxury, and were finally annihilated by the Almohads [a rival Muslim faction]. Those of them who stayed behind in the desert, remained as of old fragmented and divided. They are now in subjection to the king of the Sudan, pay him tribute, and are recruited to his army."

A West African clay sculpture depicting a snake, which was regarded as a sacred creature in many African religions. According to Soninke belief, the curse of a giant snake named Bida caused the gradual decline of ancient Ghana.

53

As Levtzion points out, Ghana most likely regained its independence and importance early in the 12th century, though the capital was moved from Kumbi Saleh to a site along the Niger. After the 12th century, however, Ghana itself largely disappeared from the Arabic chronicles. Control of the trade in that region of the Sudan passed to smaller Soninke states, principally Diara and Mena.

Ultimately, Ghana fell victim both to outside pressures and to the forces of nature. The empire survived a number of upheavals, but it could not survive the gradual exhaustion of the Bambuk goldfields during the 12th century. Significantly, oral traditions relate that after the dying snake, Bida, uttered his curse upon the Soninke, his head fell in the vicinity of Bure, the second of West Africa's three major goldfields. After the decline of Bambuk, Bure—which lies southeast of Bambuk, along the western branch of the Niger—became the main source of Sudanese gold. As the neighboring Malinke

Kwame Nkrumah (1909–72), a leader in the fight against colonialism, served as the first president of the modern nation of Ghana. Under Nkrumah's guidance, Ghana played an important role in the political and economic development of Africa.

54

people developed the resources of Bure during the 13th and 14th centuries, commercial and political power shifted to them from the Soninke. By the 14th century, Mali, the Malinke state, emerged as the great empire of the Sudan.

Fortunately, both the Arab scholars and the guardians of the Soninke tradition recorded the great days of ancient Ghana, and its legacy has lived on in Africa. In 1957, when the British colony known as the Gold Coast became the first African nation to obtain its independence, the country's leaders chose the name Ghana. Geographically, there was no relation between the two states: the modern nation of Ghana is situated on the Gulf of Guinea, hundreds of miles from the site of Kumbi Saleh, while most of the territory of ancient Ghana now lies in Mauritania and Mali. But the Africans who had just regained their freedom wished to draw symbolic power from West Africa's first great kingdom.

Under the leadership of President Kwame Nkrumah, the modern nation of Ghana embarked on an ambitious program of economic development and sought to become a positive force in African and international affairs. Primarily an agricultural nation, Ghana is now a leading exporter of cocoa and palm oil; the mining of gold, diamonds, bauxite, and manganese is also an important industry. Culturally, Ghana has developed an important film industry. Among the nation's craftspeople, Ghanaian weavers are especially known for their colorful Kente cloth, which has become popular throughout the world. In the field of education, the University of Ghana has

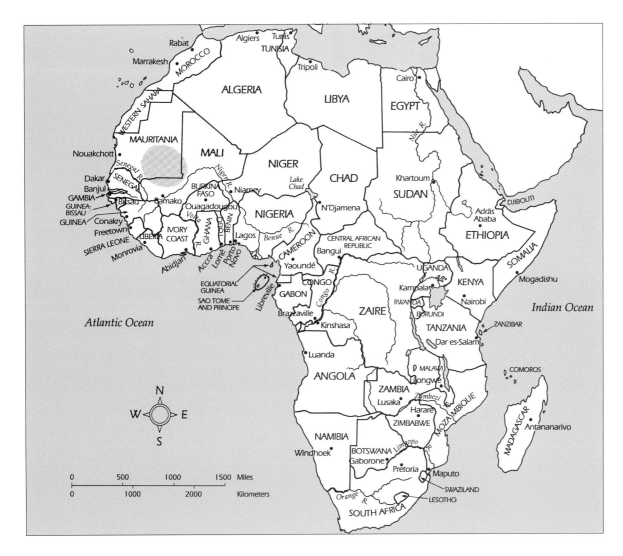

A map of contemporary Africa. The shaded area indicates the former territory of ancient Ghana.

55

played a leading role in exploring African history and archaeology. Seeking to build upon the achievements of a brilliant past, Ghana and the other nations of Africa can inspire future generations with the legacy of the Land of Gold.

CHRONOLOGY

7.5 million years ago	First hominids appear on the continent of Africa
2.5 million years ago	Stone Age begins; early humans learn to make and use tools
150,000 years ago	Modern humans emerge, most likely in Africa, and spread to other parts of the world
c. 8000 B.C.	Beginning of agriculture
c. 1000 B.C.	Beginnings of trade between farming communities in West Africa; first penetration of the Sahara by horse-drawn chariots
c. 300 B.C.	Iron Age begins in Africa; possible beginnings of trade between North Africa and West Africa; Nok culture flourishes in West Africa
c. 4th century A.D.	Camel is introduced into Africa, making the trans-Sahara journey easier
c. 500	Soninke people found the state of Wagadu

7th century	Islam sweeps through the Middle East and North Africa; trans-Sahara contacts increase
8th century	Muslims begin trading with the peoples of the Sudan; ancient Ghana emerges from the state of Wagadu and becomes the major link in the gold trade with North Africa; Kumbi Saleh grows into a prosperous city
10th–11th centuries	Ghana reaches the height of its power under Tunka Manin and other kings
1054	Almoravids conquer Awdaghust
1076	Almoravids conquer Kumbi Saleh
12th century	Ghana briefly regains its importance but soon dissolves as Bambuk goldfields are exhausted; focus of trade shifts to the empire of Mali

FURTHER READING

Bloch, Marc. *Feudal Society.* Translated by L. A. Manyon. Chicago: University of Chicago Press, 1961.

Connah, Graham. *African Civilizations.* Cambridge: Cambridge University Press, 1987.

Davidson, Basil. *Africa in History.* Rev. ed. New York: Collier, 1991.

———. *The African Genius.* Boston: Little, Brown, 1969.

———. *The Lost Cities of Africa.* Rev. ed. Boston: Little, Brown, 1987.

Davidson, Basil, with F. K. Buah and the advice of J. F. Ajayi. *A History of West Africa, 1000-1800.* New rev. ed. London: Longman, 1977.

Hourani, Albert. *A History of the Arab Peoples.* New York: Warner Books, 1991.

Hull, Richard W. *African Cities and Towns Before the European Conquest.* New York: Norton, 1976.

Kwamwena-Poh, Michael, et al. *African History in Maps.* London: Longman, 1982.

Leakey, Richard, and Roger Lewin. *Origins.* New York: Penguin, 1977.

———. *Origins Reconsidered.* New York: Anchor Books, 1992.

Levtzion, Nehemiah. *Ancient Ghana and Mali.* New York: Africana, 1980.

Levtzion, Nehemiah, and J. F. G. Hopkins. *Corpus of Early Arabic Sources for West African History.* Cambridge: Cambridge University Press, 1981.

Oliver, Roland, and B. M. Fagan. *Africa in the Iron Age.* Cambridge: Cambridge University Press, 1975.

Park, Mungo. *Travels in the Interior Districts of Africa.* Reprint of the 1799 edition. New York: Arno Press/New York Times, 1971.

Phillipson, D. W. *African Archaeology.* Cambridge: Cambridge University Press, 1985.

Previté-Orton, C. W. *The Shorter Cambridge Medieval History.* 2 vols. Cambridge: Cambridge University Press, 1952.

UNESCO General History of Africa. Vols. 1-3. Berkeley: University of California Press, 1990.

59

GLOSSARY

Almoravids   (alma-RAH-vids) a North African Muslim dynasty that flourished during the 11th and 12th centuries and conquered parts of ancient Ghana

anthropology   the study of human development, with emphasis on topics such as race, social relations, and culture

archaeology   the study of the physical remains of past human societies

descent line   also known as a clan; a group in African society united by descent from a common ancestor

feudalism   a social system, common in many parts of the world between 500 and 1500, based on the relationship between lords and vassals

ghana   "war chief" in the Mande language of the Soninke; the name by which the Soninke kingdom of Wagadu became known after the 8th century

griot   an African storyteller who preserves the oral traditions of a people

Homo sapiens   the species to which all modern human beings belong

Iron Age	the period in history, beginning about 300 B.C. in Africa, marked by the working of iron into tools and weapons
Islam	the religion based upon worship of Allah and acceptance of Muhammad as his prophet
kaya-magha	"master of the gold" in the Mande language
Muslim	one who follows the religion of Islam
oral tradition	a form of historical record in which events are passed on through generations of storytellers instead of being written down
Soninke	black West Africans who founded the states of Wagadu and ancient Ghana
Stone Age	the period of human history, beginning about 2.5 million years ago, characterized by the use of stone tools
Sudan	the region of sub-Saharan Africa stretching from the Atlantic coast to the Nile Valley; name derives from Bilad al-Sudan, Arabic for "Land of the black peoples"
vassal	a person who has accepted the protection of a feudal lord in return for a pledge of loyalty and the performance of defined services

INDEX

63

PHILIP KOSLOW earned his B.A. and M.A. degrees from New York University and went on to teach and conduct research at Oxford University, where his interest in medieval European and African history was awakened. The editor of numerous volumes for young adults, he is also the author of *El Cid* in the Chelsea House HISPANICS OF ACHIEVEMENT series and *Centuries of Greatness: The West African Kingdoms, 750–1900* in Chelsea House's MILESTONES IN BLACK AMERICAN HISTORY series.

PICTURE CREDITS